Prayers To My Father

For Jehovah is good,
his loving kindness endures forever
and his faithfulness unto all

Prayers To My Father

The Loving and Healing Power of Prayer

Jacqueline A Covington

Copyright

Copyright © 2016 by **Jacqueline A. Covington**. All rights reserved. This book or any portion thereof may not be reproduced or used in any manner whatsoever without the express written permission of Jacqueline A. Covington except for the use of brief quotations in a book review.

Printed in the United States of America

First Printing, 2016

ISBN-13: 978-1-942022-29-9

The Butterfly Typeface Publishing
PO BOX 56193
Little Rock Arkansas 72215

Dedication

This prayer journal is dedicated to my father: SFC Redger Lancaster, my children: Ayannah, Madison and Jeremiah, and my loving husband: Jeremy Covington for always being there for me.

To my mother Sandra Lancaster, my sister Rajai Lancaster and my Pastor Bishop William and Vanessa McPhaul – thank you for all you do.

*Cast down imagination and every high thing
that exalted itself against the knowledge of God
and bringing every thought into captivity
to the obedience of Christ.*

Table of Contents

Cleansing (p16)

Protection (p20)

Surrender (p24)

Marriage (p28)

Guidance (p32)

Renewal (p36)

Forgiveness (p40)

Love (p44)

Discernment (p48)

Gratitude (p52)

Freedom (p56)

Unity (p60)

Clarity (p64

Courage (p68)

Prosperity (p72)

Restoration (p76)

Purity (p80)

Burdens (p84)

Patience (p88)

Purpose (p92)

Speaking Life (p96)

A Mother's Prayer (p100)

A Church Leader's Prayer (p104)

Foreword

Prayers to My Father is a heart-felt and sincere journal filled with prayers that are relevant and needed for a time such as this.

By sharing her own hurts and desires, author Jacqueline A. Covington has managed to capture the hearts, minds and issues of our times.

Her prayers are simply written, yet packed with power. Each prayer gives the reader hope, guidance and insight into their lives.

This prayer journal blessed me and I have no doubt it will bless you as well.

Use the spaces provided to delve deep and come up with your own set of unique prayers to our Father that you can reference when needed.

He hears you and wants to ease your pain.

Iris M. Williams
Author/Publisher

Preface

Un-forgiveness can really weigh you down, keep you bound and unhappy and stop you from living the life God intended for you to live. Your vision will be so blurry that you won't be able to see the purpose God has for you.

I've always been quiet and kept to myself, but there came a time when I felt even more isolated and alone. I had low self-confidence due to my weight and how I looked. I was also dealing with issues of un-forgiveness, fear, hurt and pain.

The only thing I knew that would work was prayer. I knew I had to fall on my knees and face in prayer, calling upon God. I began fasting and praying and that's when my life began to change.

I found it comforting to write down my prayers. I decided to publish them so that others might benefit as well. I pray that these prayers are a blessing to you as they have been for me.

My prayers are specific to me and my life, but you can easily substitute certain words and make them unique to you, your life and your situation. There are extra pages inserted after each prayer for you to write down your version of the prayer we pray. Utilize the space and truly make this book your own.

To God be the Glory!

Introduction

I was raised by my step-father. My biological father wasn't in my life. I didn't understand why. I wondered if I'd done something wrong, if he loved me or just didn't want to be bothered. I struggled with forgiving him.

Through prayer, I realized that although I didn't have my biological father in my life – God had blessed me with a dad who was very special to me.

I've always had a fear of death and in 2005 when I lost my dad, it truly took me by surprise and I began to question God. Why would he take the only dad that I knew loved and cared for me? I had been taught never to question God, but it was hard dealing with the hurt and pain I felt inside.

Again, it was through prayer I learned and began to see that my dad had ran his race, fought a good fight, but he was tired and ready to go home. I still think about him often and if I had one more chance I'd tell him that I love him and that I'm thankful to have had him in my life.

Cleansing

Lord,

I ask and pray that you come see about me as I do this fast. I ask that you remove things from my life that shouldn't be there. Things that mean me no good, any sickness, any sadness, any unspoken pains. I ask that you renew in me a new heart and mind. Lord I want to be free. I give you all of me. Use me, wash me clean, and make me over. I know I have a purpose to serve, so I ask that you show me who Jacqueline is and the woman you called me to be. I ask for forgiveness and that you give me the help I need to forgive myself. Lord I ask in due time when you are ready that you fix the relationship between my mother and me. Someway show her that I love her and need her. I count this done.

In Jesus' name,

Amen.

Pray about cleansing!

✝ What things do you want removed from your life?

✝ Do you know your purpose?

✝ Are you operating in your purpose?

Jacqueline A Covington

Your Cleansing Prayer:

"Let us draw near with a sincere heart in full assurance of faith, having our hearts sprinkled clean from an evil conscience and our bodies washed with pure water"
Hebrews 10:22

Jacqueline A Covington

Your Cleansing Prayer:

"Let us draw near with a sincere heart in full assurance of faith, having our hearts sprinkled clean from an evil conscience and our bodies washed with pure water"
Hebrews 10:22

Protection

Lord,

I thank you for waking me and my family up this morning, for protecting us from any harm or danger that could have come our way, but you kept your loving arms around us and I am so thankful. Lord I'm thankful for my kids. Lord I ask that you bless me with a long life to see them grow up. Lord I ask that you send angels to each school to be with them and protect them. Lord remove any fears that keep me bound, hurts and pains that I deal with that I don't talk about. Lord am tired of feeling bound and overwhelmed. I ask that you take it away and replace it with happiness, peace, and joy. Lord fix my heart renew in me a new mind that will stay focused on you. Lord I give it all to you. Remove panic attacks. Take them away so I can be the woman you called me to be.

In Jesus' name,

Amen.

Pray About Protection!

✝ What type of protection do you need in your life?

✝ Are you tired/burdened with anything?

✝ How is it affecting you?

Jacqueline A Covington

Your Protection Prayer:

"The LORD will protect you from all evil; He will keep your soul."
Psalms 121:7

Jacqueline A Covington

Your Protection Prayer:

"The LORD will protect you from all evil; He will keep your soul."
Psalms 121:7

Surrender

Lord

I thank you this morning because it could have been the other way around. Lord I thank you for last's night rest and my upraising this morning. Lord I ask for forgiveness if I said anything or hurt anyone I ask for forgiveness. Lord I am seeking to see your face and hear your voice to speak to my heart. Lord while I'm on this fast, I ask that you separate the things from my life that mean me no good and friends that are not for me. Close all doors that need to be closed and open all doors that need to be opened. Lord I surrender my whole heart. Lord I ask if it be any sickness, you heal it. I speak good things over my life. I ask that you anoint my voice to speak into others' lives and bless them and help them come out of things so they can walk into the purpose.

In Jesus' name,

Amen.

Pray About Surrender!

- ✝ Is there something you are holding on to that you need to release?
- ✝ Have you harmed someone?
- ✝ Has someone harmed you?

Jacqueline A Covington

Your Surrender Prayer:

"Then said Jesus unto his disciples, If any man will come after me, let him deny himself, and take up his cross, and follow me. For whosoever will save his life shall lose it: and whosoever will lose his life for my sake shall find it."
Matthew 6:24-25

Jacqueline A Covington

𝒴our 𝒮urrender 𝒫rayer:

_____
_____
_____
_____
_____
_____
_____
_____
_____
_____

"Then said Jesus unto his disciples, If any man will come after me, let him deny himself, and take up his cross, and follow me. For whosoever will save his life shall lose it: and whosoever will lose his life for my sake shall find it."
Matthew 6:24-25

Marriage

Lord,

I pray that you keep us. Lord keep me in the right mind. Lord I ask that you forgive me for things that I have done or said. Lord I bring to you my marriage. Lord I ask that you fix it, Lord, I ask that you open my heart and my husband's heart to understand and listen to one another. Lord I ask that you take anger away, and forgive us for anything we said to one another that isn't pleasing in your sight. Lord I pray for a strong marriage, one that you're both in and control. Order our steps, Lord. I pray for understanding on how to be a wife. Lord, I'm seeking to hear your voice and see you work in my marriage. Lord remove fears and replace it with courage so I can overcome the fear of death. I ask that you remove it so I can live the life you would have me to live. I know we have to go, but I pray that you let me live to see my kids grow up. I know you didn't bring me this far to leave me. I shall live and not die. I have a purpose to fill and I ask that you show it to me. I speak peace, joy, happiness, increase in money, my marriage, increase in my walk with God, and increase in faith. Teach me how to love and not worry or stress over things I can't control. Lord, I give it all to you. Lord, clear my mind so I can hear from you.

In Jesus' name,

Amen.

Pray About Marriage!

- ✝ Are you in a marriage or do you have a relationship that is strained?

- ✝ Do you understand the problem(s)?

- ✝ Do you know how to exist in your marriage/relationship?

Jacqueline A Covington

Your Marriage Prayer:

_____

_____

_____

_____

_____

_____

_____

_____

_____

"Let the husband render unto the wife due benevolence: and likewise also the wife unto the husband."
1 Corinthians 7:3

Jacqueline A Covington

Your Marriage Prayer:

"Let the husband render unto the wife due benevolence: and likewise also the wife unto the husband."
1 Corinthians 7:3

Guidance

Lord,

I thank you for keeping me, ordering and guiding my steps. Lord keep my mind focused on you and the things that you would have of me. The word that comes to my mind is thankful. How thankful I am for all you have done. I lift up people that are having a hard time. I ask that you open up jobs and sources of different incomes. Lord just humble me, so I can be a blessing to someone else.

In Jesus' name,

Amen.

Pray About Guidance!

- ✝ Are you lost?

- ✝ Do you know which way to go?

- ✝ How can you bless someone else?

Jacqueline A Covington

Your Guidance Prayer:

"I will instruct thee and teach thee in the way which thou shalt go: I will guide thee with mine eye."

Psalms 32:8

Jacqueline A Covington

𝓨our 𝓖uidance 𝓟rayer:

"I will instruct thee and teach thee in the way which thou shalt go: I will guide thee with mine eye."
Psalms 32:8

Renewal

Lord,

I thank you for all you have done and are going to do. Lord I left my kids up to you this morning. Lord I ask that you carry them and keep them safe from any harm or danger that comes their way. Lord show them the true meaning of loving you and serving you. Keep them in perfect peace, Lord, show them happiness. Lord now I pray for my husband. I ask that you keep him, and protect him. Heal him from any sickness that may be going on. Lord make him the man you called him to be. Lord I ask that you fill my marriage up with your holy spirit. Lord I ask that you clear my mind of any negative things and fill it with positive things. Lord things that hurt, that I don't talk about, I ask that you remove from me, never to think about them again. Lord I owe you all the praise and a praise will forever be in my mouth.

In Jesus' name,

Amen.

Pray About Renewal!

- ✝ Are you negative?

- ✝ How do you view the world and your surroundings?

- ✝ How can you improve negative thoughts/actions?

Jacqueline A Covington

Your Renewal Prayer:

"And do not be conformed to this world, but be transformed by the renewing of your mind, so that you may prove what the will of God is, that which is good and acceptable and perfect."
Romans 12:2

Jacqueline A Covington

Your Renewal Prayer:

"And do not be conformed to this world, but be transformed by the renewing of your mind, so that you may prove what the will of God is, that which is good and acceptable and perfect."
Romans 12:2

Forgiveness

Lord,

I thank you Lord for all you've done and for waking me up in my right mind. Lord I thank you for starting me on my way. Thanks for giving me peace. Lord I ask that you continue to fill me up with your Holy Spirit and make me over. Lord I ask that you have your way. I ask that you keep me covered from anything that might come my way. I pray for healing over my family and friends. I believe and trust your word that you will and can do anything I ask. I am praying to hear your voice show me who Jacqueline really is, what you would have me to do and what my purpose is. Lord I'm seeking a healing in my heart so I can move forward, learn how to forgive, and focus more on you.

In Jesus' name,

Amen.

Pray About Forgiveness!

✝ Do you need to forgive someone?

✝ What do you need to forgive?

✝ How has not forgiving them affected you?

Jacqueline A Covington

Your Forgiveness Prayer:

"For if ye forgive men their trespasses, your heavenly Father will also forgive you: But if ye forgive not men their trespasses, neither will your Father forgive your trespasses."
Matthew 6:14-15

Jacqueline A Covington

Your Forgiveness Prayer:

"For if ye forgive men their trespasses, your heavenly Father will also forgive you: But if ye forgive not men their trespasses, neither will your Father forgive your trespasses."
Matthew 6:14-15

Jacqueline A Covington

Love

Lord,

I send up this prayer for _____. I ask that you give them peace and a desire in their heart to serve you. Lord give them the ability to think. Lord I ask that you mend the broken pieces of their heart. Take the hurts and pains and replace it with joy, happiness and love. Clean them up. Let them hear your voice, order their steps and take control of their mind so they can focus more on you.

In Jesus' name,

Amen.

Pray About Love!

- ✝ Do you need more love?

- ✝ Do you feel unloved?

- ✝ What negative thing are you replacing love with?

Jacqueline A Covington

Your Love Prayer:

"A new commandment I give unto you, that ye love one another; as I have loved you, that ye also love one another."
John 13:34

Jacqueline A Covington

Your Love Prayer:

"A new commandment I give unto you, that ye love one another;
as I have loved you, that ye also love one another."
John 13:34

Discernment

Lord,

Please come into my heart. I need you to fix things that are hurting me or keeping me bound. Lord give me an open heart and mind to serve your word no matter what. Lord heal the little girl so that I can become the woman you called me to be. Teach me how to be a wife, a mother and a true friend. Lord I'm seeking your face and your voice. Protect and guard my heart from anything not like you.

In Jesus' name,

Amen.

Jacqueline A Covington

Pray About Discernment!

- ✝ Can you hear the voice of God?
- ✝ Is your mind open?
- ✝ What is God saying to you?

Jacqueline A Covington

Your Discernment Prayer:

"My sheep hear my voice, and I know them, and they follow me"
John 10:27

Jacqueline A Covington

𝒴our 𝒟iscernment 𝒫rayer:

"My sheep hear my voice, and I know them, and they follow me"
John 10:27

Gratitude

Lord,

I'm so grateful for all you have done and are going to do. Lord I thank you for mending the relationship between my mother and me. Lord I ask that you keep her covered from any harm or sickness. I speak healing over her life, her mind and any hurts that she's dealing with, I ask that you heal and take them away. I also pray that you teach me how to love myself first so I can love others. Lord show me how to protect my heart from brokenness and bitterness. I ask that you cover me with you blood. Lord keep my mind focused on you. Any thoughts not like you, take them away, never to return again. Empty me God. I'm an open vessel seeking to hear from you. I'm praying for a true encounter with you. Give me a worshipping spirit. Let your anointing fall and rest over my life.

In Jesus' name,

Amen.

Pray About Gratitude!

† What are you grateful for?

† What do you need to release in order to allow gratitude to dominate your life?

† What are you focused on?

Your Gratitude Prayer:

"Cease not to give thanks for you, making mention of you in my prayers;"
Ephesians 1:16

Jacqueline A Covington

Your Gratitude Prayer:

"Cease not to give thanks for you, making mention of you in my prayers;"
Ephesians 1:16

Freedom

Lord,

Please give me freedom, peace, joy, and happiness. Give me the abilities to speak your word in someone else's life. Show me the plan you have for my life. I pray to be more in touch with your word. Teach me how to wait on you. Lord, I ask that you stop the chatters in my mind. I am free and saved, so devil move! I send you back to where you came from never to return or bother me or my family again, so I can move forward and be happy with my life and family. I have been bound too long and I'm calling you out! I count it done.

In Jesus' name,

Amen.

Pray About Freedom!

† Are you free? If not, why?

† If so, how do you know?

† Who or what is keeping you from being free?

Jacqueline A Covington

Your Freedom Prayer:

"Stand fast therefore in the liberty wherewith Christ hath made us free, and be not entangled again with the yoke of bondage."
Galatians 5:1

Jacqueline A Covington

Your Freedom Prayer:

"Stand fast therefore in the liberty wherewith Christ hath made us free, and be not entangled again with the yoke of bondage."
Galatians 5:1

Unity

Lord,

Thank you for keeping me and my family. Lord I ask that you give my family peace, happiness and bring us back together so we can love one another. Lord let them hear and see your word for themselves because we need you. I lift my cousin up in prayer to you Lord, be with her. She's dealing with hurts and pains. Lord I ask that you be with her, let her know your still there and you hear her cries. Let her know that you forgive her. She's lost, confused and needs you. Please Lord don't leave her. I lift her mother up. They're in a place where they have never been before. Lord be with her, wrap your loving arms around her. I speak healing over this situation she shall be free, and her mind will stay on you. I count it done.

In Jesus' name,

Amen.

Pray About Unity!

- ✝ Do you have peace in your life?

- ✝ How important is peace to you?

- ✝ What needs to happen in order for you to find peace?

Jacqueline A Covington

Unity Prayer:

"Peace I leave with you, my peace I give unto you: not as the world giveth, give I unto you. Let not your heart be troubled, neither let it be afraid."
John 14:27

Jacqueline A Covington

Unity Prayer:

"Peace I leave with you, my peace I give unto you: not as the world giveth, give I unto you. Let not your heart be troubled, neither let it be afraid."
John 14:27

Clarity

Lord,

I pray to be able to focus on you and your word. Order my steps and focus my mind on you. Change my mind and mindset so I can think for myself, so I can go free and bring my family out. I see now I'm nothing without you and your word. I cry out. I need you to come see about me. I'm praying for understanding, Lord. Remove fears and stress and place positive people in my life so I can focus. Keep all things that come to destroy away so I can live according to your word, so my life can line up according to your will and I can stay focused and stand fast on your word.

In Jesus' name,

Amen.

Jacqueline A Covington

Pray About Clarity!

✝ Is your mind constantly racing?

✝ Are you able to focus on the things you need to make a priority?

✝ What is causing stress in your life?

Jacqueline A Covington

Your Clarity Prayer:

―――――――――――――――――――――――――
―――――――――――――――――――――――――
―――――――――――――――――――――――――
―――――――――――――――――――――――――
―――――――――――――――――――――――――
―――――――――――――――――――――――――
―――――――――――――――――――――――――
―――――――――――――――――――――――――

"Let this mind be in you, which was also in Christ Jesus:"
Philippians 2:5

Jacqueline A Covington

Your Clarity Prayer:

"Let this mind be in you, which was also in Christ Jesus:"
Philippians 2:5

Courage

Lord,

I ask that you remove all people from my life that mean me no good and that pray against me. Keep confusion and trouble away, so I can have peace. Lord I see now that I can't do anything without you. Lord I pray for peace. I know joy comes from you and only you. Lord hear my cries. I need you. Wash me clean from the top of my head to the bottom of my feet. Free my mind, break my chains and set me free. Clear my mind so I can hear from you. Lord, take all fears away and build me up to be the woman you called me to be. Lord, show me how you would have me to bring peace and show me their purpose.

In Jesus' name,

Amen.

Pray About Courage!

- ✝ What are you afraid of?

- ✝ What happens if your fears become a reality?

- ✝ What would you do if you were not afraid?

Jacqueline A Covington

Your Courage Prayer:

"Fear thou not; for I am with thee: be not dismayed;
for I am thy God: I will strengthen thee; yea, I will help thee;
yea, I will uphold thee with the right hand of my righteousness."
Isaiah 41:10

Jacqueline A Covington

Your Courage Prayer:

"Fear thou not; for I am with thee: be not dismayed; for I am thy God: I will strengthen thee; yea, I will help thee; yea, I will uphold thee with the right hand of my righteousness."
Isaiah 41:10

Prosperity

Lord,

As I lay in front of you, I ask that you bless everyone that is in need and crying out. Lord, give them peace. Show them in some kind of way that you are there and that you hear them. Let them know that everything will be ok. Lord people are struggling in their minds. I ask and speak healing over them. I speak blessings over their lives. Lord they need you. Lord I ask that you send protection around their homes and families. Lord bless them going out and coming in, increase their money, and Lord I ask that you give them understanding and let them think for themselves.

In Jesus' name,

Amen.

Pray About Prosperity!

✝ What are you *crying out for*?

✝ What happens if what you are *crying out for* becomes a reality?

✝ Does *crying out* mean you don't have faith?

Jacqueline A Covington

Your Prosperity Prayer:

"In my distress I called upon the LORD, and cried to my God for help; He heard my voice out of His temple, and my cry for help before Him came into His ears. Then the earth shook and quaked; and the foundations of the mountains were trembling and were shaken, because He was angry..."
Psalms 18:6-7

Jacqueline A Covington

Your Prosperity Prayer:

"In my distress I called upon the LORD, and cried to my God for help; He heard my voice out of His temple, and my cry for help before Him came into His ears. Then the earth shook and quaked; and the foundations of the mountains were trembling and were shaken, because He was angry..."
Psalms 18:6-7

Restoration

Lord,

Restore in me you. Fill me up with your holy spirit. Release anything that's not like you. Lord I need you to come see about me. Lord give me positive thoughts. Let my mind stay focused on you and your will. Lord I'm here to serve to with my heart. Close all doors that might be open that's not like you and open doors that need to be opened. Lord I confess that I am saved and I owe you all the glory. Lord give me and others understanding so we can do your will.

In Jesus' name,
Amen.

Pray About Restoration!

- ✝ What has you weighted down?

- ✝ How do you know that you're weighted down?

- ✝ Once God has restored you, what will be different in your life?

Jacqueline A Covington

Your Restoration Prayer:

"Now the God of hope fill you with all joy and peace in believing, that ye may abound in hope, through the power of the Holy Ghost."
Romans 15:13

Jacqueline A Covington

Your Restoration Prayer:

"Now the God of hope fill you with all joy and peace in believing, that ye may abound in hope, through the power of the Holy Ghost."
Romans 15:13

Purity

Lord,

I need thee right now to come see about me and my family. Change my thought life and change my mind set. Lord forgive me for my sins and thoughts. Lord come speak to my heart and clean my mind. I speak good things over my life and my children lives, peace, joy and happiness. Lord I pray you let me live a long life because my kids need me and I need them. Lord remove all fears and strongholds from my life and their lives, never to be heard of or seen again. Lord send special angels to be with my children at school and home. Send an angel to be with my daughters Madison and Ayannah. I call them queens and I call them blessed and saved and women of God. I ask that you send an angel to be with my son, Jeremiah, Lord. I call him saved and I speak good things over their lives. I ask that you anointed them to speak your word and also live by it.

In Jesus' name,

Amen.

Pray About Purity!

† What are your prayers for your child(ren)?

† What blessings do you speak over their lives?

† Why is it important to speak things as if they were already so?

Jacqueline A Covington

Your Purity Prayer:

"And all thy children shall be taught of the Lord; and great shall be the peace of thy children."
Isaiah 54:13

Jacqueline A Covington

Your Purity Prayer:

"And all thy children shall be taught of the Lord; and great shall be the peace of thy children."
Isaiah 54:13

Burdens

Lord,

I ask that you give me peace in my mind and healing. Lord I pray for focus. Lord I ask that you stop the chatters in my mind so I can hear a word from you. Open my ears to hear what you would have me to hear and to live according to your will. Lord show me how to out think the chatters so I break out of the bondage that keeps me bound and tied up in my mind. I believe it and count it done.

In Jesus' name,

Amen.

Pray About Burdens!

- ✝ What are *chatters*?

- ✝ How can you stop the *chatters*?

- ✝ What do you run the risk of happening, if you allow the *chatters* to continue?

Jacqueline A Covington

Your Burdens Prayer:

"But avoid worldly and empty chatter, for it will lead to further ungodliness, and their talk will spread like gangrene."
2 Timothy 2:16-17

Jacqueline A Covington

Your Burdens Prayer:

"But avoid worldly and empty chatter, for it will lead to further ungodliness, and their talk will spread like gangrene."
2 Timothy 2:16-17

Jacqueline A Covington

Patience

Lord,

I want to thank you for keeping me in my right mind and good health. Lord this worrying spirit that I have, I ask that you remove it. Lord I ask that you give me a clear mind to think and focus on you and the things that you have planned for my life because Lord I don't mind waiting on you. Lord touch my heart. Renew in me a new spirit. Lord I'm waiting on you. Open my ears and eyes to be able to hear and see your word and bless me to be able to see my purpose. I am so grateful for everything, so I don't mind waiting on you Lord.

In Jesus' name,

Amen.

Jacqueline A Covington

Pray About Patience!

- ✝ What are you worried about?

- ✝ Have you done all you can do about the situation?

- ✝ What prevents you from waiting 'patiently' on the Lord?

Jacqueline A Covington

𝒴our 𝒫atience 𝒫rayer:

_____

_____

_____

_____

_____

_____

_____

_____

_____

"Wait on the LORD: be of good courage, and he shall strengthen thine heart: wait, I say, on the LORD."
Psalms 27:14

Jacqueline A Covington

Your Patience Prayer:

"Wait on the LORD: be of good courage, and he shall strengthen thine heart: wait, I say, on the LORD."
Psalms 27:14

Jacqueline A Covington

Purpose

Lord,

Please remove all fears and close all doors to fear, fear of death, fear of not being loved, sickness, fear of not being wanted or fitting in. Close the doors to all those fears that keep others bound. Close all these doors so I can walk into my calling and know my purpose so I can be the woman you called me to be. Lord remove the fear of worrying, unhappiness, and being sad. You didn't give us the spirit of fear, but of power, love and a sound mind, so I claim good things over my life and my family's lives. No longer will I be bound, but free with a free mind and peace.

In Jesus' name,
Amen.

Pray About Purpose!

- ✝ Are you afraid to fail or are you afraid to succeed?

- ✝ What happens if your fears become a reality?

- ✝ What would you do if you were not afraid?

Jacqueline A Covington

𝓨our 𝓟urpose 𝓟rayer:

_____

_____

_____

_____

_____

_____

_____

_____

_____

"For God hath not given us the spirit of fear; but of power,
and of love, and of a sound mind."
2 Timothy 1:7

Jacqueline A Covington

𝒴our 𝒫urpose 𝒫rayer:

"For God hath not given us the spirit of fear; but of power, and of love, and of a sound mind."
2 Timothy 1:7

Speaking Life

Lord,

Please teach me how to think before I speak. Teach me how to use my tongue for good and not evil to bring others down. Lord, lead and guide me to do what is right. I have learned that the tongue can be a dangerous thing and that the power of life and death lies in the tongue so watch what you speak over your life and others. I declare and decree I shall live and not die and that I'm a child of God my father who sits high and looks low. All things are possible through him. I speak joy, happiness, and peace. I shall be forgiven and I shall forgive. I am grateful and I speak all good things over my life and my family. My kids shall be saved and strongholds shall be broken. Depression has got to go and fear also. I'm closing all doors because what God has for me it is for me.

In Jesus' name,

Amen.

Pray About Speaking Life!

✝ What things are you speaking negatively about?

✝ Why are you speaking negatively?

✝ How can you change your behavior?

Jacqueline A Covington

Your Speaking Life Prayer:

_____

_____

_____

_____

_____

_____

_____

_____

_____

"Death and life [are] in the power of the tongue:
and they that love it shall eat the fruit thereof."
Proverbs 18:21

Jacqueline A Covington

Your Speaking Life Prayer:

"Death and life [are] in the power of the tongue:
and they that love it shall eat the fruit thereof."
Proverbs 18:21

Jacqueline A Covington

A Mother's Prayer

Lord,

I lift my kids up to you, asking you to cover and protect them from any evil any doors that have opened. I ask that you close them so it doesn't affect my kids' lives. Lord teach me the true meaning of being a mother. Show me Lord. I want to raise them up to do right and live according to your word. Lord I count it done.

In Jesus' name,

Amen.

Jacqueline A Covington

Pray A Mother's Prayer

- ✝ Can you pray for your children even if they are grown?

- ✝ Can you pray for your child(ren) even if they don't want to change?

- ✝ Will your prayers be effective, or heard?

Jacqueline A Covington

Your Mother's Prayer:

"As one whom his mother comforteth, so will I comfort you; and ye shall be comforted in Jerusalem."
Isaiah 66:13

Jacqueline A Covington

𝒴our ℳother's 𝒫rayer:

"As one whom his mother comforteth, so will I comfort you; and ye shall be comforted in Jerusalem."
Isaiah 66:13

Prayers To My Father 103

Jacqueline A Covington

Church Leaders

Lord,

I thank you for my pastor and bishop. Lord I'm standing here praying for them. I ask that you continue to keep them lifted up so they can do your will and be vessels of your word. Lord continue to anoint their voices so they can speak your word and bless others.

In Jesus' name,

Amen.

Pray About Church Leaders!

✝ Do church leaders need your prayer?

✝ What reasons would you pray for your church leader(s)?

✝ What blessings do you wish for your leader(s)?

Jacqueline A Covington

Your Church Leaders Prayer:

"Let him that is taught in the word communicate unto him that teacheth in all good things."
Galatians 6:6

Jacqueline A Covington

Your Church Leaders Prayer:

"Let him that is taught in the word communicate unto him that teacheth in all good things."
Galatians 6:6

Conclusion

There was a time when I felt down on myself and unhappy because of my weight gain. The devil would bring to my mind sickness. I always thought something was wrong with me and that I wasn't normal which caused me to continue to be unhappy and sad.

With prayer and love, I started declaring happiness and joy over my life, freedom for my family, and today I am happy.

I am learning to be who I am and not who others feel I should be. I stopped trying so hard to get everybody else's approval and started living for God instead, because nobody has a heaven or hell to place me in but GOD.

I believe that the devil only attacks people who have a purpose or a calling in their lives. I have learned that the devil doesn't play fair; he comes to steal, kill, and destroy. My Pastor always said, "The devil comes when you're alone."

This book means a lot to me because these prayers are personal and come straight from my heart. There were times when all I could do was be alone. I couldn't pray out loud, but I could write. This prayer book helped me make it through. I pray that these prayers bless you as they have blessed me.

So like I said before the devil doesn't play fair, but I'm here to tell you that there is power and love to be found in prayer!

About the Author

Born to Redger and Sandra Lancaster, and raised in Fayetteville NC, twenty-nine-year-old Jacqueline Alexandria Covington is the oldest of two children. Her younger sister is named Rajai Lancaster. The Covingtons currently lives in Raeford NC.

Married to her loving husband, Jeremy Covington for nine years, the two have three children; Ayannah (age 9), Jeremiah (age 7) and Madison (age 4).

Jacqueline's hobbies are reading, spending time with her children, going to church and singing.

Covington graduated from Hoke County High School in 2005 and is currently enrolled in college.

As the wife of a minister, Jacqueline understands the importance of praise and worship. The family attends New Beginnings Praise and Worship Church in Raeford North Carolina. The Bishop is William McPhaul and the Pastor is Dr. Vanessa McPhaul.

"Faith is important because I want to live right according to Gods will. I want to treat others the way I want to be treated."

Mrs. Covington is employed at Preferred Care in Raeford North Carolina. Her goals for the future include living right, helping others and being the best wife and mother she can be.

She also plans to write more self-help books.

No weapon formed against me shall prosper…

The Butterfly Typeface Publishing

Contact us for all of your
publishing & writing needs!

Iris M Williams
PO Box 56193
Little Rock AR 72215

www.butterflytypeface.com

www.ingramcontent.com/pod-product-compliance
Lightning Source LLC
Chambersburg PA
CBHW081458040426
42446CB00016B/3300